T0050991

How does a BONE become a FOSSIL?

Revised Edition

Melissa Stewart

capstone

©2010, 2016 Raintree
an imprint of Capstone Global Library, LLC
Chicago, Illinois

To contact Capstone Global Library, please
call 800-747-4992, or visit our web site
www.mycapstone.com

All rights reserved. No part of this publication may be reproduced or transmitted in any form or by any means, electronic or mechanical, including photocopying, recording, taping, or any information storage and retrieval system, without permission in writing from the publisher.

Edited by David Andrews and Laura Knowles
Designed by Richard Parker and Wagtail
Original illustrations © Capstone Global Library, LLC 2010
Illustrated by Jeff Edwards

Picture research by Hannah Taylor and Sally Claxton
Originated by Modern Age Repro House Ltd

Library of Congress Cataloging-in-Publication Data is available on the Library of Congress website.
ISBN 978-1-4109-8529-3 (revised paperback)
ISBN 978-1-4109-8376-3 (ebook)

Image Credits

Alamy: blickwinkel, 6, Tim Cuff, 28; Capstone Press: Jeff Edwards, 8, 10-11; Getty Images: Sovfoto, 23; iStockphoto: gfrandsen, 20, microgen, 26; Newscom: David R. Frazier/DanitaDelimont.com, 17, lbum/Tolo Balaguer, 29, Tony Waltham/robertharding, 7; Reuters: 27; Science Source: 16, Christian Jegou/Publiphoto, 4; Shutterstock: AlessandroZocc, 18, Christian Darkin, 21, Elenarts, 12, Frank Bach, 13, Ken Wolter, 22, Maria Arts, 24, Matteo Chinellato, 25, Pi-Lens, Cover Bottom, siraphat, Cover Top, Vladimir Sazonov, 15, Volodymyr Goinyk, 19; SuperStock: Wolfgang Kaehler, 5; Thinkstock: Stockbyte, 14

Every effort has been made to contact copyright holders of any material reproduced in this book. Any omissions will be rectified in subsequent printings if notice is given to the publisher.

All the Internet addresses (URLs) given in this book were valid at the time of going to press. However, due to the dynamic nature of the Internet, some addresses may have changed, or sites may have changed or ceased to exist since publication. While the author and Publishers regret any inconvenience this may cause readers, no responsibility for any such changes can be accepted by either the author or the Publishers.

Printed in the United States 4409

Contents

Signs of Past Life 4
Two Kinds of Fossil 6
From Fish to Fossil 8
Buried Treasure 10
Where Fossils Form 12
Common Body Fossils 14
Dinosaur Fossils 16
Molds and Casts 18
Traces of the Past 20
Trapped in Tar and Ice 22
What Is Amber? 24
Scientists at Work 26
Be a Fossil Hunter 28
Glossary 30
Find Out More 31
Index 32

Some words are shown in bold, **like this**. You can find out what they mean by looking in the glossary.

Signs of Past Life

Long ago, our world was a very different place. Life was only present in the oceans and no animals or plants lived on land.

Eusthenopteron was a genus (group of similar types) of fish that swam in the sea about 385 million years ago. Its name means "strong fin."

This painting shows a variety of animals that lived in Earth's oceans 300 to 700 million years ago.

Back-up breathing

Eusthenopteron had a big advantage over other fish. It could breathe in two different ways. Most of the time, it took in the gas oxygen through its gills. But it also had sacs that worked like lungs to get extra oxygen from the air. Animals need oxygen to live and grow.

The last *Eusthenopteron* died millions of years ago. This kind of fish disappeared long before the first humans lived. It became **extinct** long before the age of dinosaurs, too.

If you want to know what *Eusthenopteron* looked like, you can go to a museum. But do not expect to see bodies with fins and scales. After millions of years, the bodies are long gone. All that remains are **fossils**, or pieces of evidence of this ancient life.

Eusthenopteron fossil

Eusthenopteron lived in oceans all over the world. This fossil was found in Miguasha National Park in Quebec, Canada.

Two Kinds of Fossil

Scientists study **fossils** to find out how creatures lived long ago. They also find out how life on Earth has changed over time.

Body fossils are the remains of plants, animals, and other creatures that were once alive. Dinosaur bones, shark teeth, and seashells are all body fossils. So are **petrified** trees (trees that have turned to stone) and leaf **imprints**. These fossils show us what life was like millions of years ago.

Fossilized shark teeth show us that sharks have lived in Earth's oceans for millions of years.

Shark teeth

Dinosaur footprints

A scientist examines part of the world's longest dinosaur trackway. It is located in Bolivia, a country in South America.

Trace fossils tell us something about how ancient creatures lived. Dinosaur footprints, **coprolites** (animal droppings), and vomit are all trace fossils. So are tooth marks and stomach stones, unhatched eggs, and ancient animal homes. These fossils help us understand how ancient creatures moved, what they ate, and how they raised their young.

Many scientists study body fossils and trace fossils together. That gives them the clearest picture of the ancient world.

From Fish to Fossil

Dead *Eusthenopteron* sank to the muddy seafloor. Although soft body parts rotted away, hard bones were left behind.

A fish's bones have a lot in common with our bones. They help a fish move and also protect its soft body parts.

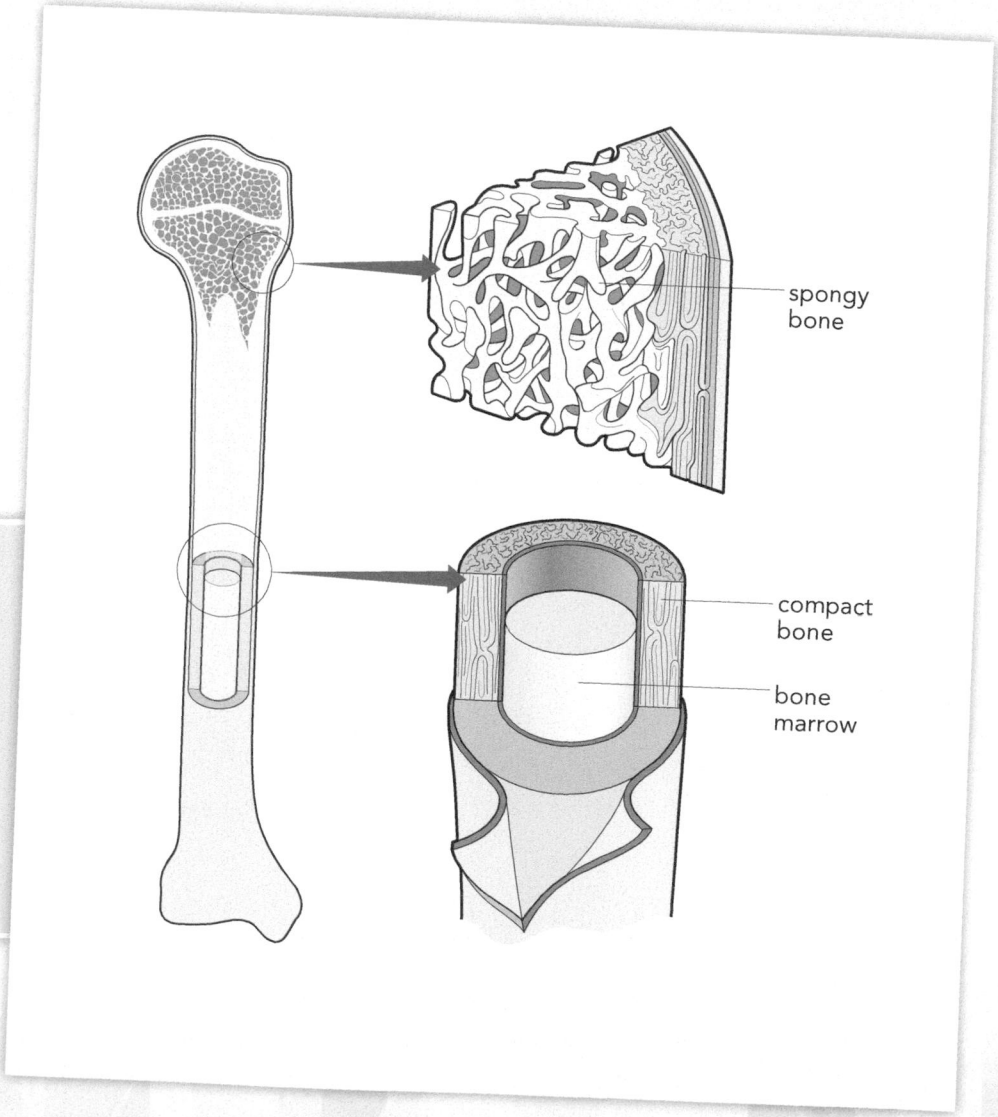

Many animals' bones have a hard outer layer and are softer on the inside.

Most bones have two layers. Hard **compact bone** is on the outside. It is made up of rings of **minerals** (natural solid materials). The softer inside layer is called **spongy bone**. It is full of tiny holes that contain bone marrow, a kind of tissue. New blood cells are made in the bone marrow.

Like bone, water contains lots of minerals. When bones are surrounded by water for a long time, minerals in the water replace the original bone.

Over millions of years, minerals from ocean water took the place of the minerals in *Eusthenopteron* bones. Then they hardened to form **fossils**. The hard stone looked just like *Eusthenopteron* bones.

Magical fossils?

In the past, people did not understand how fossils form. Some people thought fossils were magical rocks that could keep milk fresh, bring good luck, or ward off evil spirits.

Buried Treasure

While *Eusthenopteron* **skeletons** were turning into **fossils**, layers of mud and sand piled up on top of the bones. The weight of the top layers pushed down on the lower layers.

Over millions of years, this fish's skeleton becomes a fossil. If the fossil is exposed, people can dig it up and study it.

Over time, the mud and sand stuck together. Then they hardened to form rock. The fish fossils were trapped deep underground.

As more time passed, the land around the fossils changed. An earthquake may have shifted the land and brought some fossils to the surface.

Wind or water could have slowly eroded (worn away) the rock above other fossils. After millions of years, parts of fish fossils stuck out of the ground.

People noticed *Eusthenopteron* fossils and dug them up. Then scientists studied the fossils to find out when *Eusthenopteron* lived and how it survived.

What's in a name?

Scientists who study fossils are called **paleontologists**. The word *paleontologist* comes from a Greek word that means "those who study ancient things." The word fossil comes from a Latin word that means "dug up."

Where Fossils Form

Tyrannosaurus rex is one of the largest meat-eating dinosaurs scientists have found.

Modern humans have lived on Earth for about 200,000 years. But dinosaurs ruled the land for 165 million years.

How many dinosaurs lived during all that time? Billions of them existed, but most of them did not leave behind **fossils**. Many dead dinosaur bodies, including the bones, were eaten. Others rotted away.

For a fossil to form, the conditions had to be just right. The body of a dead creature had to be covered with mud or sand soon after it died. The built-up layers of mud, sand, and other materials—called sediment—protected the **skeleton** from the sun, wind, and rain.

Most fossils are found in rock that was once underwater. That is why the most common fossils are the remains of ocean creatures.

Petrified logs, Arizona

These petrified logs were once part of a giant forest that grew in Arizona.

Fossil forests

Bone is not the only material that can turn to stone. **Petrified** Forest National Park in Arizona contains thousands of logs that became fossils after their wood was replaced by **minerals**. Scientists think the huge trees died about 225 million years ago.

Common Body Fossils

Scientists have discovered many **fossils** of fish bones. But shark teeth are the easiest **body fossils** to find. Why? Because there are so many of them.

A shark's teeth grow in rows. When a tooth falls out, the one behind it moves to fill the space.

Sharks have lived on Earth for 450 million years. They are constantly losing old teeth and growing new ones. A shark may lose up to 10,000 teeth in its lifetime. That is a lot of teeth!

Ammonites first lived in Earth's oceans around 240 million years ago. Like lobsters and snails, ammonites were **invertebrates** (animals without a **spine** or other bones). Their soft bodies were surrounded by hard, spiral-shaped shells. Today, ammonites are long gone. But people often find fossils of their hard shells.

These ammonite fossils formed as layers of limestone built up around them. Limestone is made of the crushed shells of tiny ocean creatures.

Ammonite fossils

More than 10,000 kinds of **trilobites** lived in the ocean 540 million years ago. The last of these invertebrates died about 250 million years ago. But people find fossils of their hard outer coverings in rocks all over the world.

Scientists have also found many ancient fossils of sea stars, sea urchins, clams, and scallops.

Dinosaur Fossils

When someone says the word **fossil**, you probably think of dinosaurs. Maybe you have even seen models of *Tyrannosaurus, Triceratops, Seismosaurus*, and other giant beasts at a museum. But did you know that scientists have discovered fossils from fewer than 3,000 dinosaurs in the whole world?

Most of the dinosaur fossils **paleontologists** have dug up come from small animals. But some are bigger than a bus. Imagine what it would be like to discover one of them.

A scientist works carefully to unearth a dinosaur at Dinosaur National Monument in Utah.

That is what happened to a U.S. fossil hunter named Susan Hendrickson. In 1990 she spotted some bits of bone fossils in a cliff in South Dakota. They were part of the largest and most complete *Tyrannosaurus rex* ever found. Today, the dinosaur, named Sue, is on display at the Field Museum of Natural History in Chicago, Illinois.

'Sue' the Tyrannosaurus rex

Can you imagine how excited Susan Hendrickson must have been when she discovered this giant dinosaur?

Did you know?

Seismosaurus is the longest dinosaur ever found. It could grow as long as four school buses parked end to end. The giant plant eater lived in the western part of North America about 145 million years ago.

Traces of the Past

What can scientists learn from **trace fossils**? They can learn all kinds of things.

- **Coprolites** and vomit tell us where and when animals lived and what they ate.

Dino droppings

In 1995 a Canadian **fossil** hunter named Wendy Sloboda found a huge coprolite in Canada. It was the size of two loaves of bread placed end to end. Scientists think it may have been left behind by a *Tyrannosaurus rex*.

Coprolites come in different shapes and sizes.

Coprolites

- Ancient dinosaur nests show us how many eggs the dinosaurs laid at one time and how much care the parents gave their young.
- A trail of dinosaur footprints helps us understand how an animal moved, how tall it was, and how much it weighed.

This computer artwork of a dinosaur protecting its nest from a predator could not have been made without the information learned from trace fossils.

Protoceratops guarding its eggs

- Giant stone termite mounds in Gallup, New Mexico, help us understand how the ancient insects lived.
- Tooth marks provide clues about how prehistoric predators (animals that kill other animals) hunted, and what they ate.
- Stomach stones show us where plant-eating dinosaurs lived and how they digested their food.

Trapped in Tar and Ice

About 65 million years ago, all the dinosaurs on Earth became **extinct**. That meant **mammals** could take over all the places where dinosaurs had lived. (A mammal is an animal that has a **spine** and feeds its young with mother's milk.) Over time, mammals grew larger and larger. They spread out all over the world.

Just like dinosaurs, mammals left behind **fossils**. Scientists have discovered some mammal fossils in rock. Others have been found in some very strange places.

Rancho La Brea Tar Pits, Los Angeles

These model mammoths show how animals became trapped in tar long ago.

In the early 1900s, people started to pull fossils of woolly mammoths, saber-toothed cats, giant ground sloths, and early horses out of the Rancho La Brea Tar Pits in Los Angeles, California. All these animals had lived about 40,000 years ago. They died when they were trapped in large, shallow puddles of thick, sticky tar.

Discovery of a baby mammoth

In 1989, workers pulled this baby mammoth out of the icy ground in northern Russia.

Scientists working in Russia have found several woolly mammoths trapped in ice. Some of the fossils still have skin, hair, and soft inner organs. Scientists think these mammoths died when mudflows quickly buried the animals. Over time, layers of ice built up around the bodies and froze them.

What Is Amber?

Some ancient trees oozed a thick, sticky liquid called **resin**. Over millions of years, the resin dried and hardened to form **amber**.

Some modern trees ooze sticky, golden resin, too.

Oozing resin

Amber is a beautiful yellowish-brown material that some people use to make jewelry. Sometimes amber contains bits of plants or tiny creatures that got stuck in the resin.

Scientists have found chunks of amber with flies, ants, mosquitoes, spiders, and small worms inside. They have even discovered pieces of amber that contain small frogs and lizards.

In 2001 a U.S. scientist named Lynn Margulis accidentally dropped a piece of amber with a 20-million-year-old termite inside. Since the amber was broken, she decided to drill into tiny bubbles near the termite's body and see what was inside. She found ancient gas produced by bacteria—tiny, one-celled creatures—living in the termite's gut.

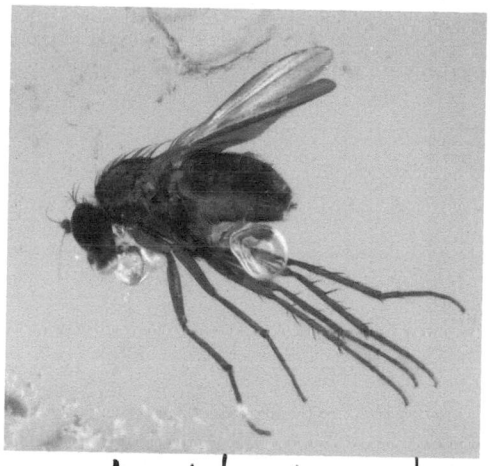

A midge in amber

This tiny midge got itself into a sticky situation about 40 million years ago. Today, it is preserved in amber.

The oldest feathers

Scientists know that the first birds lived about 150 million years ago. But until 2000, the only sign of their feathers were **imprints**. That is when scientists working in France found seven feathers stuck inside a 100-million-year-old piece of amber. They are the oldest feathers on Earth.

Scientists at Work

This scientist is using small tools to carefully chip away at the rock surrounding a fossil.

To find **fossils**, scientists go to deserts and other places where plants do not cover the ground. They look for rocks that formed millions of years ago. Then they hunt for bits of bone and other signs of fossils in the rock.

When the scientists spot something, they take measurements and make drawings of the area. Then they start digging.

At first, workers use axes, shovels, and jackhammers to break open the rock. When they get close to the fossil, scientists use small tools to chip away tiny pieces of rock. They work slowly and carefully for hours, days, or even weeks.

Finally, the scientists cover the fossil in a pasty material called plaster and lift it out of the ground. The plaster dries and hardens to protect the fossil while it travels back to the laboratory. Then the scientists study the fossil closely.

This scientist is working on a fossil that has been protected with a layer of plaster.

Did you know?

In the 1870s, scientists working in Colorado and Wyoming found many large dinosaur fossils. That is when people in the United States started to become interested in ancient life on Earth.

Be a Fossil Hunter

Fossils are easier to find than you might think. No matter where you live, there are probably some fossils nearby. There might even be some in your neighborhood. The next time you see a rock, pick it up and look at it closely. Can you see a fossil inside?

A family hunt for fossils on a beach in Great Britain.

Fossil hunting

You probably will not find a dinosaur bone, but you might spot some shark teeth or small sea animals. Once you learn how to look for fossils, you can find them almost anywhere.

An Ichthyosaurus fossil

Ichthyosaurus fossils have been found in North and South America and Europe.

Kids can do it!

Sometime around 1811, when Mary Anning was about 12 years old, she discovered the first *Ichthyosaurus* fossils near her home in Lyme Regis, England. *Ichthyosaurus* was a large reptile that lived in the ocean.

To get started, call local museums. Ask them to suggest some good places to look for fossils. They might even offer field trips for fossil hunters.

If you find a fossil, a field guide can help you identify it. If you think it is a really interesting fossil, contact a **paleontologist**. You never know what you might find.

Glossary

amber dried, hardened resin (the sticky liquid some plants produce)

ammonite invertebrate with a spiral-shaped shell. Ammonites lived in the ocean around 240 million years ago.

body fossil remains of plants, animals, and other creatures that were once alive

cast fossil that forms when minerals harden inside a mold

compact bone hard outer surface of all bones. Some bones contain only compact bone.

coprolite fossilized animal dropping

extinct die out or disappear from Earth forever

fossil any evidence of ancient life

imprint shape sometimes left in built-up layers of mud, sand, and other materials before a bone rots

invertebrate animal with no spine or other bones

mammal animal that has a spine and feeds its young with mother's milk

mineral natural solid material

mold fossil of an imprint

paleontologist scientist who studies fossils

petrified turned to stone or another hard substance

resin thick, sticky liquid some plants produce for protection from insects

skeleton all the bones that make up an animal's body

spine bones that run down an animal's back and support it

spongy bone soft, flexible tissue inside some bones

trace fossil evidence of how an ancient creature lived

trilobite invertebrate with a hard outer covering. Trilobites were common in Earth's oceans for millions of years, but disappeared about 250 million years ago.

Find Out More

Books to read

Do you still have questions about bones and fossils? There is much more to learn about these fascinating topics. You can find out more by picking up some of these books from your local library:

Arnold, Caroline. *Global Warming and Dinosaurs: Fossil Discoveries at the Poles*. New York: Clarion, 2009.

Kudlinski, Kathleen V. *Boy, Were We Wrong About Dinosaurs!* New York: Puffin, 2008.

Sloan, Christopher. *Bizarre Dinosaurs: Some Very Strange Creatures and Why We Think They Got That Way*. Washington, D.C.: National Geographic, 2008.

Internet Sites

FactHound offers a safe, fun way to find Internet sites related to this book. All of the sites on Facthound have been researched by our staff.

Visit *www.facthound.com*

Index

amber 24–25
ammonites 15
Antarctica 19

bacteria 25
birds 25
body fossils 6, 7, 14–15
bone marrow 8, 9
bones 8–9
breathing 4
Britain 18, 28, 29

Canada 5, 20
casts 18
clams 15
compact bone 8, 9
coprolites 7, 20

dinosaur footprints 7, 21
Dinosaur National Monument 16
dinosaurs 5, 6, 12, 16–17, 19, 20, 21, 22, 27

eggs 7, 21
Eusthenopteron 4–5, 8, 9, 10, 11
extinction 5, 22

ferns 19
field guides 29
fish 4–5, 8, 11
fossil formation 9, 12–13, 18
fossil hunters 17, 20, 26–29

Ichthyosaurus 29
imprints 6, 18, 19, 25
insects 21, 25
invertebrates 15

La Brea Tar Pits 22, 23
leaf imprints 6, 19
limestone 15

mammals 22
mammoths 23
minerals 9, 13, 18
molds 18

nests 21

oxygen 4

paleontologists 11, 16, 29
Petrified Forest National Park 13
petrified trees 6, 13
Protoceratops 21

resin 24
Russia 23

saber-tooth cats 23
seashells 6, 15
sediment 12
Seismosaurus 17
shark teeth 6, 14, 28
skeletons 12
sloths 23
spines 15, 22
spongy bone 8, 9
stomach stones 7, 21

termites 21, 25
tooth marks 7, 21
trace fossils 7, 20–21
Triceratops 16
trilobites 15, 18
Tyrannosaurus rex 12, 16, 17, 20

United States 13, 16, 17, 22, 23, 27

vomit 7, 20